Jon Swindall

Bunny in the winter

illustrated by
Galyna Vasylyshyn

Bunny in the winter.

Bunny doesn't like the cold.

Bunny in the winter...

puts on more clothes.

Red shirt. Sweatshirt.
Anything warm.

"It's cold. It's COLD.
IT'S COOOOOLD!"
cries Bunny.

It's too bad
these earmuffs don't fit me
anymore.

She cries a tear...as
she fears...she will never
be warm again.

What`s Bunny to do?

Not Give Up!
That's What!

Hop

So I will hop

to stay warm.

Yes - I will hop hop HOP to stay warm.

HEY, BUNNY!

Please, Bunny,
don't shiver anymore.

Go inside and close the door!

You don't have
to be cold anymore!

The End

Made in the USA
San Bernardino, CA
23 November 2019